TRUE VALOR

Stories of Brave Men and Women
in World War II

Publisher: Jack Artenstein
Vice President/General Manager,
Juvenile Division: Elizabeth D. Amos
Director of Publishing Services: Rena Copperman
Project Editor: Michael Artenstein
Managing Editor: Jessica Oifer
Art Director: Lisa-Theresa Lenthall
Typesetter: Brenda Leach/Once Upon a Design

Library of Congress Catalog Card Number: 95-50392

ISBN: 1-56565-458-7

Lowell House books can be purchased at special discounts when ordered in bulk for
premiums and special sales. Contact Department JH at the following address:

Lowell House Juvenile
2029 Century Park East, Suite 3290
Los Angeles, CA 90067

Manufactured in the United States of America

10 9 8 7 6 5 4 3 2 1

Contents

Introduction

History teaches us that war is an unfortunate yet unavoidable reality of human life on earth. When individuals, groups, or nations seek power and control over others, the result—whether localized or widespread—is often an armed conflict.

In the middle of the twentieth century two nations pursued their dreams of global power and domination in separate parts of the world: Germany in Europe, and Japan in the Pacific. The result of these actions was World War II.

In his quest for *lebensraum* (living space) for Germany, Adolf Hitler easily conquered most of Europe between 1936 and 1940. The Germans allied with Italy and Japan—then attacked their former ally in the war, the Soviet Union. By 1941, Great Britain and Russia stood alone against the German war machine.

In the Pacific, the Japanese had similar plans for expansion and empire. After conquering Manchuria and most of China in the late 1930s, Japan launched a surprise attack on the American Navy fleet at Pearl Harbor, Hawaii. The United States finally entered the war against Japan and its ally, Germany, in December 1941.

It took over a year before American military might and manpower reached their full potential. By early 1943, the tide began to turn against both the Germans and the Japanese. The Allies (America, Great Britain, and the Soviet Union) slowly took back island after island in the Pacific, as well as regions across Europe.

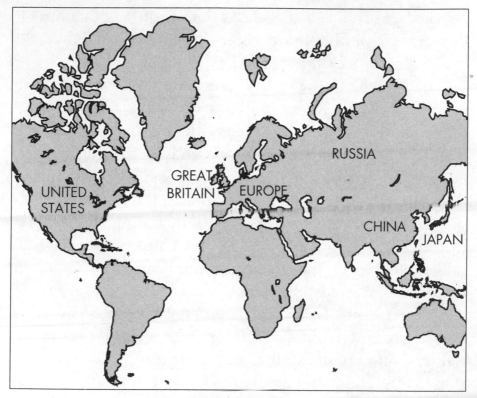

World Map

Hitler's dreams of a German world order died with him in his Berlin bunker in May 1945. Three months later, the Japanese surrendered after the United States dropped a new weapon—the atomic bomb—on the Japanese cities of Hiroshima and Nagasaki.

World War II formally ended on September 2, 1945. One of the results of the conflict was the widespread destruction of Japan, much of Europe, Russia, and all of Germany. Reconstruction of these areas became a top priority for the victors of the war.

Carried out by Hitler and his Nazi party, the Holocaust, in which six million innocent people were exterminated, shocked the civilized world. As details of the Nazi atrocities became public knowledge, people around the world recoiled in horror and disbelief.

The two chief powers to emerge from the war were the United States and Russia, with the Russian Soviets occupying much of Eastern Europe. With the dropping of the atomic bombs on Japan, the world entered the nuclear age. For the first time in history, the possibility of global destruction became a reality. More than thirty million people lost their lives in World War II, including those killed in the Nazi Holocaust. The Soviet Union alone lost 20 million people. Of the 16 million Americans who served in the War, 405,399, lost their lives.

Germany and Japan were ultimately defeated by ordinary men and women. Uniformed soldiers, resistance fighters, and civilians all risked their lives to take a firm stand for freedom and liberty.

The history of World War II is replete with stories of courage and heroism both on and off the battlefield.

Much has changed since the end of World War II. The governments of Germany and Japan are now among our strongest allies and supporters. Today, these countries take their rightful places among the democracies of the world.

A Shot in the Dark

In the 1930s, Germany's Adolph Hitler used anti-Semitism (hostility toward Jewish people) to unite the German people against those whom Hitler deemed the common German enemy. As the leader of the Nazi party, Hitler blamed the Jews for much of the country's long-standing problems. His "final solution" to the Jewish problem was genocide, the widespread and systematic extermination of an entire race. The execution of more than six million Jews by the Nazis in World War II makes this one of the darkest periods in human history.

In the early 1940s, as German military forces conquered much of Europe, Hitler began transporting Jews from all over the continent to concentration camps in Poland. The Jews from the Netherlands (Holland) were no exception. The Germans occupied the entire country by May of 1940, and by the war's end in 1945, it was estimated that over 80 percent of the Jewish population in the Netherlands had been killed (about 115,000 out of 143,000 people).

There were few hiding places in this small, flat country and no easy escape routes, since the Netherlands was surrounded by Germany to the east, occupied Belgium to the south, and the North Sea to the north.

Many brave men and women of the Netherlands nevertheless risked their lives to help the Jews. Marion Van Binsbergen was one of them.

Marion Van Binsbergen

When twenty-three-year-old Marion Van Binsbergen heard the pounding on the door of her large country

Northern Europe

house, her pulse quickened, and her mind went numb with fear. It was late at night, and she had a pretty good idea who was standing on the other side of the front door—and why.

Immediately she thought about the children—five-year-old Lex, three-year-old Tom, and thirteen-month-old Erica—sleeping beneath the living room floorboards with their father. She wondered if they, too, had heard the banging and whether they were as frightened as she was.

Two more heavy knocks sounded from the front door, echoing like thunder through the quiet house.

Marion had grown fond of the Pollack family over the months, especially the children. But now it seemed that the worst of her fears had come true—the childrens' lives were in danger. She sat in the dark and listened to the sound of her heart beating against her chest.

Marion flashed back to an experience that she'd had over a year ago while in Amsterdam, the capital of the Netherlands. It was this incident that led to her decision to join the Resistance movement. She was riding a bicycle down a canal one afternoon when she heard screams and cries up ahead. As she approached the scene, she saw six or seven children standing in the street next to several German soldiers. The oldest child appeared to be around eight years old, the youngest, no more than two. The soldiers were loading the children into the back of an army truck. Those who resisted were grabbed by the hair and forced inside. Marion stood some twenty feet away, watching as the last child, the youngest, was hoisted aboard. The fear in the child's eyes made Marion shudder: She knew she was powerless to alter the children's unspeakable fate.

Like the vanishing image of the child in the truck, the memory of that horrible day had gradually faded from Marion's mind. But now it was back, as vivid as ever. Only this time the little girl on the back of the truck reaching out to Marion was young Erica Pollack.

Marion now sat motionless in bed, staring into the black as though searching for some distant light, a flash or flicker of hope.

Again there was the banging on the front door. She steeled herself and rose from her bed, the contours of the furniture now coming into grim focus.

The children's mother had died shortly after baby Erica was born. Their father, Freddie Pollack, had done his best to keep the family together, but soon after the Nazis arrived, news came that Jews were being deported from Holland. Freddie Pollack, himself a Jew, then sought out the help of the Dutch Resistance, an underground group that fought in secret against the German occupation. Freddie had heard that the Resistance often helped Jews hide or escape from the Germans. It was his only hope.

The woman Freddie met from the Resistance was a close friend of Marion Van Binsbergen, and she persuaded Marion to hide the Pollack family.

"Open the door or we'll break it open," a voice boomed in German.

Then another: "Open up, Miss Van Binsbergen. We know you're home!"

Wringing her hands, Marion moved slowly, robotically, out of her room and toward the front door.

Please let the children remain quiet, she thought, flicking on the hall light. *Please let them stay quiet.* The walk to the front door took forever.

"I'm sorry it took so long," she explained. "I must have been in a deep sleep."

Four German officers and a member of the Dutch Nazi party stood on the porch, staring at Marion inquisitively. She immediately noticed that the Germans were dressed in black, and her heart began to beat a little faster. These Germans were Secret Service, also known as the Gestapo, the most brutal and feared officers in the German military. It was common knowledge that those prisoners taken by the Gestapo rarely, if ever, returned.

The Dutch Nazi spoke first. "Are you hiding any Jews, Miss Van Binsbergen?" He was a small, heavyset man, with a thick mustache and a pug nose.

Marion ignored the lump in her throat and looked the man straight in the eyes. "Of course not," she insisted, lifting her head just perceptibly, as if in defiance.

The Dutch Nazi gave a smug look to his four colleagues and then stepped through the threshold of the front door. "Then I assume you won't mind my having a brief look around."

"No, not at all."

The four Germans never moved. They remained, as though chiseled from gleaming onyx, perfectly statuesque in their black uniforms—chins up, hands clasped behind their backs, their eyes focused dead straight ahead. Their stern, merciless presence was almost too much for Marion to bear.

Marion stood on the front porch next to the SS officers and tried her best to appear calm. But she soon began to worry. What was that Dutch Nazi doing in there? Had he found the Pollacks? Several minutes went by before she had an answer.

"Miss Van Binsbergen?"

She turned to see the stout Dutch Nazi now standing in the doorway.

"No Jews here," he said.

When the Nazis finally left, Marion closed the door behind her and almost fell to the floor with relief. Moments later she heard baby Erica's muffled cries. "It's okay, kids," Marion said. "You can come out now." The Pollacks emerged from the secret trapdoor and immediately thanked Marion for what she had done on their behalf.

They were standing in the center of the living room, sobbing and holding on to one another, when the front door burst open, and the Dutch Nazi walked in.

"I thought so," he said, grinning broadly.

Marion and the Pollack family stood motionless, their terrified faces frozen as if captured in a still photograph. The Nazi closed the door and took several steps toward the group.

"We get so many Jews this way." He shook his head from side to side and smacked his lips. "Come with me."

"Please, they're only children," Marion pleaded.

"They're no concern of yours," the man snarled. He moved forward and grabbed Freddie Pollack by the arm. "My German brethren will be most interested to see all of you—including you, Miss Van Binsbergen."

The children began to sob, and Marion suddenly felt overcome by the moment. She imagined the children being hoisted into the back of an army truck, and suddenly the blood seemed to rush out of her legs. She had only one chance.

Moving with deliberate calm, she backed into a small table in which she kept a loaded pistol.

Summoning up every last shred of nerve, she opened the drawer, took out the pistol, and pointed it straight at the Nazi.

"Don't move!" she yelled.

The Nazi turned with a bemused look on his face. "Come, now, Miss Van Binsbergen. Give me the gun."

"If—if you take the children," she stammered, "you'll die."

"They're Jews," he said, coming slowly toward her,

one arm outstretched and beckoning for her to hand over the gun.

The gunshot wasn't as loud as Marion had imagined it would be. The Pollack family froze.

In his last few seconds alive on earth, the Nazi's dumbfounded expression never changed. He stood there, midstride, looking down at the blood that suffused the front of his uniform. He coughed twice and then fell to the floor, like a puppet suddenly released from its master's grip.

"I had no choice," Marion mumbled, looking down at the dead man by her feet, tears trickling down her cheeks. "I wish there had been some other way."

Freddie Pollack and his children then rushed to her side. But both Marion and Freddie knew they had no time to waste. Their work was not yet finished. They had to get rid of the Nazi's body before others came looking for him.

The children kept watch by the front window as Marion and Freddie wrapped the body in a blanket and took it down to the cellar. Marion then contacted the village undertaker, a man who happened to be a member of the Resistance, a man she could trust.

That same night the undertaker picked up the body and disposed of it by placing it in a coffin alongside another body.

By some stroke of luck, the Gestapo never traced the Dutch Nazi's disappearance back to Marion's house.

The Pollacks survived.

When the war finally ended in 1945, Marion Van Binsbergen said good-bye to the Pollack family. But they weren't the only Jewish family she helped. Through her efforts in hiding and placing Jews in safe homes, Marion Van

Binsbergen saved more than 150 Jews from certain death at the hands of the Nazis.

In 1947, Marion met and married an American named Tony Pritchard. They both now live in Vermont, where she is a practicing psychoanalyst. Baby Erica remained in Amsterdam and became a psychologist. She is the mother of three children. Marion visits her regularly.

Marion Van Binsbergen's story is told in the book *Rescuers* by Gay Block and Malka Drucker.

Yad Vashem, the Holocaust memorial in Jerusalem, Israel, recognizes non-Jews who took action to save lives during World War II. In 1983, Yad Vashem honored Marion Van Binsbergen-Pritchard as a rescuer who demonstrated moral courage during the Holocaust. She was presented with a bronze medal that is inscribed with the following words:

"Whoever saves
a single life
is as one
who has saved
an entire world."

ACE

At the beginning of World War II in the Pacific, the Japanese met with little resistance from the United States and its Allies. They quickly captured the British colonies of Singapore, Malaya, and Hong Kong in Southeast Asia, as well as American-controlled islands such as Guam, Wake, Corregidor, and the Philippines. The only bright note for America in the early days of the war was a successful bombing raid over Tokyo, Japan's capital, in April 1942.

By late spring of that year, the United States succeeded in breaking secret Japanese communication codes. An enemy plan to attack Midway Island, an important point in the Americans' line of defense and a gateway to the Hawaiian Islands, was discovered.

When the Japanese attacked Midway on June 4, 1942, the Americans were ready and waiting. Wave after wave of fighter planes attacked the Japanese fleet whose planes were still lined up on carrier decks waiting to take off. The United States routed the Japanese fleet and they retreated westward.

The Allies went on the offensive, and step by step retook Japanese-held islands and territories. In the Battle of the Philippine Sea in mid-1944, U.S. planes shot down more than three hundred Japanese fighters and sank three enemy carriers, losing less than thirty of their own aircraft.

The Battle of Midway was the turning point in the war in the Pacific and clearly proved the importance of air power in modern warfare. This successful air war against enemy forces was a key factor in the eventual defeat of the Japanese Empire.

Major Gregory "Pappy" Boyington

Major Gregory Boyington and his squadron of twenty-four F4U Vought Corsair fighter planes circled watchfully high above the main Japanese base of Kahili in the Solomon Islands of the South Pacific. As American bombers unloaded their payload of bombs at an elevation of 10,000 feet, not a single Japanese fighter came up to challenge them.

It was October 17, 1943, and the war in the Pacific had slowly turned in America's favor. The Allies were gradually taking back territory from the Japanese, island by island.

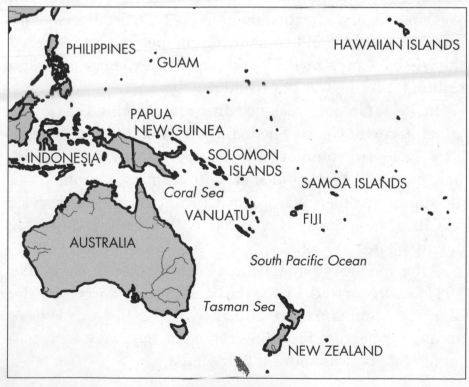

South Pacific

In the air, American planes like the Corsair were challenging the Japanese Zeros, and coming out on top.

The men of Marine Squadron 214 called Gregory "Pappy" or "the old guy." At thirty-one years of age he was the oldest active Marine fighter-pilot and would most likely not be allowed another tour of duty. Known as the "Black Sheep," the squadron was formed by Gregory from other units' rejects and replacements.

Gregory was a hotshot, and he believed he could break Captain Eddie Rickenbacker's World War I record of twenty-six enemy kills. But there was more to the brash pilot than his cocky exterior.

Gregory Boyington was born on December 4, 1912, in Coeur D'Alene, Idaho. He was raised near Okanogan, Washington, and attended the university in Seattle. Gregory received a degree in aeronautical engineering and entered the Marine Corps in 1935. Although an excellent pilot and skillful leader, he was brash and rowdy.

In 1941, Gregory resigned from the Marine Corps and joined General Claire Chennault's Flying Tigers in China. This American volunteer group of pilots provided the Chinese army of Chiang Kai-shek with training, supplies, and air support in their war against Japan. During his service in China, Gregory was credited with shooting down six enemy planes.

After the Japanese attack on Pearl Harbor in December 1941, he returned to the United States to rejoin the Marines. Months passed, and it wasn't until Gregory sent an angry telegram to the Secretary of the Navy in Washington that he was allowed to re-enlist.

Assigned to the Central Solomon Islands from September 12, 1943, to January 3, 1944, it was here that Gregory formed the legendary "Black Sheep Squadron" that became the most feared air unit in the Pacific.

Always a character, Gregory relaxed in the cockpit of his plane on long bomber escort flights. Joseph Schott, author of *Above and Beyond*, described how Gregory would use rubber bands and string attached to his flight controls to create a type of automatic pilot that allowed him to take short naps.

According to Schott, protective members of the Black Sheep would keep a sharp lookout when "the old guy . . . [was] . . . taking a nap." Gregory also had his own security system for nap time. If a wing dropped or rose, Gregory would touch a rubber band and the plane would even out. If the plane went up or down, the change in the sound of the engine would wake Gregory up and he would level off the plane.

On January 3, 1944, Gregory and his squadron, flying at twenty thousand feet over Rabaul, New Britain Island, went after several Japanese planes below them. Gregory shot down one plane, then two more before he suddenly found himself surrounded by Zeros. Diving at full speed to escape, he pulled out only a hundred feet above the water when his main gasoline tank exploded in flames. Without opening his canopy, Gregory ejected right through the glass and parachuted into St. George's Channel off the Japanese-held island.

While Gregory floated in plain sight, four enemy planes swooped down and fired at him. Miraculously they missed their target. Just before dark, a Japanese submarine took the badly wounded Gregory prisoner. When his identity was discovered, the Japanese purposely refused him medical treatment because he had so often humiliated them in air combat over the Solomons. Gregory barely survived his

Many believe a pilot's skill is measured by the number of enemy aircraft he shoots down. A running total of kills was kept by most fliers in World War II as well as by the press. The pressure to break Rickenbacker's World War I record of twenty-six kills was very intense. Although Pappy Boyington was the top Marine Corp ace of World War II, his total of twenty-eight kills was exceeded by men in other branches of the service.

In the Army Air Corps, a friendly rivalry developed between pilots Dick Bong, Tommy McGuire, and Neal Kearby. Kearby's luck ran out in October 1943, when he crashed his plane and died.

Bong went on to break Rickenbacker's record, and when he accumulated twenty-eight planes shot down, he was ordered back to the states for a rest. McGuire had twenty planes shot down to his credit and hoped to catch up with Bong. Unfortunately, he had a bout of malaria, and by the time he recovered, he was still eight behind his rival.

On January 7, 1945, while attempting to protect a plane in his squadron from attacking a Japanese Zero, McGuire's airplane stalled in a high-speed vertical banking (curved) maneuver. He was killed when the plane crashed before he could bail out. McGuire received the Medal of Honor posthumously.

Dick Bong, America's leading fighter ace of World War II, spent the remainder of the war stationed in the United States and married his high school sweetheart. On August 6, 1945, a P-80 jet fighter plane he was flying stalled shortly after take-off and crashed, killing the twenty-four-year-old instantly.

injuries and was flown to a prison camp in Yokohama, Japan.

Classified as missing in action and presumed dead, Gregory Boyington was awarded the Congressional Medal of Honor and described as a "superb airman and determined fighter against overwhelming odds."

When the war ended in 1945, Gregory "Pappy" Boyington turned up alive in the Yokohama prison camp. In addition to the Medal of Honor, he also received the Navy Cross.

Gregory never thought of himself as a hero. He once said, "Show me a hero and I'll show you a bum." He, nevertheless, accepted his award with honor, changed his legal name to "Pappy" in 1962, and died at the age of seventy-six in 1988.

A Teenager in Combat

In August of 1939, Germany and Soviet Russia (the USSR) signed a ten-year nonaggression pact, each country pledging neutrality to the other in case of war. The agreement also prohibited either country from attacking the other or joining an association of powers aimed at the other. But the agreement didn't last. Within two years Hitler saw the Soviet Union as the only obstacle standing in his way of total control of the European continent.

Operation Barbarossa, the code word for Germany's invasion of the USSR, began in June 1941. Three million German soldiers pushed across the Russian border along a front line that extended more than 1,100 miles from the Arctic region to the Black Sea. The Nazi war machine crushed the ill-equipped and ill-prepared Soviet armies, and by late October, the Germans were positioned outside the capital city of Moscow.

But the Russians refused to give up. Despite incredibly high losses, the Soviet people rallied and fought back. With help from a bitterly cold winter, the Russians finally stopped the Nazi advance. And by early 1943, they counterattacked, defeating the German 6th Army at Stalingrad and forcing the Nazis to retreat. This was Hitler's first significant defeat and the turning point in the war.

Katyusha Mikhalova

When the flotilla of Soviet marines rushed onto the beach from their landing craft, the German defenders opened fire. The marines were forced to swim inland while

Russia

German machine gunners aimed at their foreheads. The continuous spray of enemy fire made the bubbling water seem as if it were boiling. Most of the island's low-lying banks were flooded, and the Soviets kicked and thrashed through water that quickly rose above their heads.

It was December of 1944, and as the Russian armies moved west toward Berlin, the German capital, the marines were ordered to take part in an important battle in Yugoslavia. The strategically built fortress of Iluk was located on an island in the middle of the Danube River near the city of Vukovar. The marines' task was to land on a nearby island to divert German fire long enough for a

Russian land force to take the fortress. The landing took place at night, but few had anticipated the treacherous flood.

Eighteen-year-old Katyusha Mikhalova, the only female member of the flotilla, swam for her life along with the rest of her comrades. Trained as a nurse, Katyusha carried a medical bag along with her grenades and machine gun. Katyusha would not abandon the wounded who were bleeding and drowning in the icy water around her. They were her friends and companions, and she was determined to rescue as many as she possibly could.

In the distance, Katyusha saw a small piece of elevated land and desperately began to pull the wounded men toward it. As reported by Shelley Saywell in her book *Women in War*, Katyusha described what happened in her own words. "I dragged each one up," she said, "and tied them with my bandages or their belts to the tree branches that were above water."

The Germans quickly surrounded the small piece of dry land. The wounded marines begged the Russian teenager to blow them up with one of her grenades. "Better to kill us now, Katyusha, than let us be slowly cut to pieces by the Germans," they pleaded.

"Never," declared the teenager. "I'll never give up as long as there's breath left in my body!"

Katyusha was true to her word. She continued to care for the wounded men even as dawn came, and the enemy could easily make out their positions. Suddenly a shot rang out, and a German bullet tore into the young girl's shoulder artery. Katyusha passed out from the loss of blood and pain.

"When I regained consciousness," she said many years later, "the Germans were very close—only ten feet away. I took an antitank grenade from my belt and threw it at them. . . . Our cook took several grenades and jumped toward them, dying instantly."

When Katyusha had no grenades left, she grabbed her machine gun and began shooting at the enemy. The Germans surrounded the Russian girl and her wounded companions and opened fire. Katyusha had no idea how long she continued to fight using her comrades' guns and ammunition.

The fortress at Iluk was finally conquered by Russian troops later that afternoon. Of the nearly one hundred members of the flotilla who took part in the landing, only the eighteen-year-old and twelve others were still alive. Katyusha had singlehandedly killed fifty-six German soldiers and was responsible for saving the lives of all of her surviving comrades.

After her ordeal, twenty-two shell fragments were removed from Katyusha's torn shoulder, and she then became ill with pneumonia. The courageous young woman recovered sufficiently to continue serving with the marines until the end of the war in May 1945.

According to the author Saywell, the teenage girl was recommended for the title of Hero of the Soviet Union by her commander after the battle of Iluk. But the generals in Moscow turned her down. Despite the commander's testimony, they simply could not believe that a young girl could have accomplished what was claimed.

Katyusha Mikhalova was a remarkable young woman. Like thousands of Russian women, she learned at an early age that when one's homeland is threatened, every able-bodied citizen, regardless of sex or age, is needed to fight. That was exactly the situation on June 22, 1941, a warm sunny morning, when war suddenly descended upon the unsuspecting Russian people.

Katyusha was a tiny fifteen-year-old girl on her way to visit her older brother for the summer. The pale blond teenager was the youngest of three parentless children who had spent most of their lives in an orphanage.

When the train that she was traveling on neared the Russian city of Smolensk, which is southwest of Moscow, the first German bombs began falling from the sky, effectively ending the nonaggression pact signed by Hitler and Stalin in 1939. Katyusha recalled those first moments of the war in Saywell's book. "There was chaos and screaming," she said. "I . . . saw bodies everywhere. I looked for the little girl who had been sitting with me. I found her body trembling, but her head had been blown off. . . ."

Along the two-thousand-mile Russian border, German troops were crushing the Russian army and advancing toward major cities such as Leningrad and Moscow. Katyusha was stranded in Smolensk and tried to enlist as a nurse, since she had Red Cross training. The recruiting officer turned her away. "You belong in kindergarten," he said.

Two weeks later, with the city of Smolensk under attack, the desperate commander of a rifle unit gave Katyusha a uniform and a weapon. In no time, Katyusha found herself on thirty-mile-a-day marches carrying a heavy pack, a gun, a shovel, and a medical bag. Her regiment was immediately sent north to help in the defense of Moscow.

In the first months of the war, the Russian forces retreated from the advancing Germans. But as the weather turned bitterly cold, the Russians dug in and took a stand against the invaders. But in early 1942, Katyusha was seriously wounded in the leg by an exploding shell. The doctor wanted to amputate, but the young girl refused. The doctor agreed reluctantly, and Katyusha recovered after several months away from the front lines—her leg intact.

In the summer of 1942, Katyusha was assigned to a naval medical ship and was involved in the battle of Stalingrad. Katyusha's ship traveled up the Volga River to evacuate the city's wounded. When the Germans bombed the medical ship, it sank in the icy waters of the Volga. Hundreds of the wounded drowned. ". . . I don't remember much," Katyusha recalled, "but they tell me I was rescued when I was near the bottom of the sea. When I was in the hospital, a nurse told me I was born lucky."

At the age of seventeen in late 1943, Katyusha received the Order of the Patriotic War during a night marine attack on Kerch'El'tigen, which took place during a terrible storm. The brave teenager rescued many of the wounded, carrying men who were more than twice her weight and size out of the water and onto land. There, she tended their wounds and engaged in hand-to-hand fighting when it was necessary.

After recovering from shoulder wounds she sustained in the Battle of Iluk in Yugoslavia, Katyusha was with her unit when the war finally ended on May 9, 1945. "I began to cry," she remembered. "I threw down my gun and said, 'I will never pick one up again'!"

The nineteen-year-old veteran returned to her home in Leningrad to discover that her brother and sister, the only remaining members of her family, had been killed in action.

Katyusha had survived major battles and suffered serious injuries during the war only to face more suffering when she returned home. One million people had starved to death in Leningrad while Katyusha was away. "The final battle that we faced together," she declared, "was hunger!"

Each year since 1945, the Russian people have celebrated the end of World War II. The Russian women who participated in what is now called the "Great Patriotic War" turn out for the celebration bearing their medals pinned to the front of their dresses. Now they look like grandmothers, not battle-wise soldiers. They carry purses, not guns. They stand proudly, shedding tears for their fallen comrades and remembering the days when they valiantly fought for their homeland.

Nearly one million Russian women volunteers served in combat positions during World War II. Although officer policy prohibited females from engaging in battle, the Russian military was caught so off-guard by Germany's 1941 surprise attack that women were readily accepted into the service despite the regulations. They served in the air force, on tanks, in artillery units, and as medics.

The Russian military specially trained women as snipers in the field. Their job was to shoot at individual enemy soldiers from a hidden or long-range position. Russian military officers believed that women were the best snipers because they were more patient than men and would wait longer for an ideal shooting opportunity.

The Sinking of the U.S.S. *Tang*

While American land forces concentrated on defeating Germany in Europe, U.S. submarines in the Pacific took their toll of Japanese mechant ships and naval vessels. Some 250 submarines participated in the American war effort. U.S. naval power sent tons of enemy shipping to the ocean's bottom, including more than 200 Japanese warships. In fact, the Japanese military later attributed their defeat in World War II to the effectiveness of U.S. submarines.

Those volunteers who manned submarines made up less than two percent of the Navy's total personnel, yet suffered the highest casualty rate in all of the armed forces. The specific mission of the "silent service"—so nicknamed for the top-secret nature of its operations—was to "execute unrestricted . . . submarine warfare against Japan."

Commander Richard H. O'Kane

T he men who could walk shuffled to their work detail in the prisoner-of-war (POW) camp on Omori, an island near Yokohama, Japan. In tattered, dirty clothes, with rags for shoes, they resembled the walking dead.

Few had the strength to dig the large caves that the Japanese used as bomb shelters and food-storage areas. Most were afflicted with diseases such as hepatitis, dysentery, or beriberi. Many had open sores that wouldn't heal.

The 300-calories-per-day diet, which consisted mainly

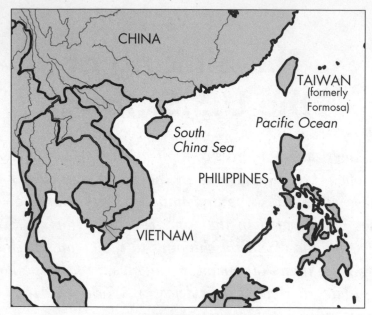

Southeast Asia

of watery soup and stale rice, had transformed these once-healthy servicemen into mere shadows of their former selves. Most weighed less than one hundred pounds.

Among them was Officer Richard O'Kane, naval academy graduate and commander of the submarine U.S.S. *Tang.* O'Kane and seven members of his crew were captured ten months earlier while patrolling the waters of the Formosa Strait, the body of water between Taiwan and mainland China.

As Commander O'Kane began digging beneath the sweltering August sun, his mind returned to that fateful day aboard the *Tang.*

"We've got a convoy of enemy ships on radar, Captain!" shouted the duty chief's messenger.

Commander O'Kane rushed to the conning tower and eyed the nine blips on the radar screen. "Let's go with a night surface attack," declared O'Kane. "They'll never know what hit them."

The first officer sounded the sub's alarm bells. "Stand by for battle surface!" he shouted.

The *Tang* was several thousand yards ahead of the convoy and still undetected. "All slow," ordered O'Kane.

O'Kane's plan was for the ships of the convoy to overtake the *Tang*. The *Tang* would attack the two lead tankers and a freighter at the front of the convoy. The crew waited breathlessly. As the seconds passed they worried about whether the lead ships would detect their presence behind them.

"We're in range, Captain," said the first officer. "Anytime now."

"Constant bearing," replied O'Kane, one eye glued to the conning tower. There was utter silence, then O'Kane gave the command all were waiting to hear. "Fire!"

Five electric torpedoes fired in succession at the enemy vessels. The crew members stood frozen as the torpedoes made their deadly underwater runs. Suddenly several large blasts punctured the silence of the submarine.

"Direct hits, Captain," reported the first officer. "They're afire and sinking."

O'Kane didn't have time for congratulations, though. An enemy transport opposite the tanker had spotted the *Tang*.

"They're going to ram us," yelled the first officer. "One hundred yards and closing."

A barrage of bullets from enemy guns crackled all around the *Tang*'s deck and bridge. "Left full rudder," O'Kane shouted only thirty seconds before the collision.

The *Tang*'s sudden swing to starboard somehow

brought the submarine alongside the enemy transport. In fact, the *Tang* was so close that gunners on the deck of the Japanese ship above them could not lower their guns enough to get a clear shot at the personnel on deck!

As the *Tang* pulled away from the transport, O'Kane prepared to give the order to dive, but held back when he spotted another enemy freighter closing in from the opposite side. "Right full rudder," screamed O'Kane. As the *Tang* maneuvered out of the way, the two ships headed for a collision with each other.

"Open torpedo doors," O'Kane ordered. "Fire one. Fire two. Fire three. Fire four."

The commander had experienced his share of dangerous manuevers before, but none quite like this. "All ahead full," he declared. "Get her out of here fast!"

Seconds later there were four tremendous explosions. The freighter went down instantly, and the transport was crippled in the water. All five major ships of the convoy had been sunk or disabled.

• • • • •

After spending the day submerged, the *Tang* resurfaced the next night, October 24, looking for action.

"Another convoy, Captain, and it's a big one," exclaimed the duty chief's messenger. O'Kane counted fourteen major ships and twelve smaller escorts to the right and left of the main column on the radar screen.

"Ready torpedo tubes," ordered O'Kane. "Prepare to fire."

As the ships in the convoy approached, they were carefully tracked by the *Tang* personnel.

Suddenly two destroyer escorts pulled out of the column firing bursts of antiaircraft fire into the air. "They're on to us, Captain," reported the first officer. "We're under attack."

O'Kane waited. The air was filled with gunfire. "Constant bearing, Mark," he shouted. "Fire first torpedo."

Seconds passed and five more torpedoes were on their way to enemy targets. The crew waited in silence, waiting to hear confirmation that the underwater bombs had found their marks. They didn't have to wait long. In less than a minute, a series of loud explosions shook the submarine.

The gunfire continued, but now the night sky was ablaze with fire from the burning enemy ships. A tanker and destroyer had burst into flames, and the transport lay disabled in the water.

"Right full rudder. All ahead one third," ordered O'Kane. The *Tang* pulled away from the scene and returned after about an hour to finish off the crippled transport so that the enemy couldn't salvage her cargo.

The *Tang*'s twenty-third torpedo of the patrol was fired in a straight line nine hundred yards from the transport. Seconds later torpedo number twenty-four was on its way.

To the horror of O'Kane and the others on the bridge, the last torpedo malfunctioned. It abruptly broke to the surface only yards ahead of the *Tang*'s bow, turned sharply left, and then began to circle back.

"All ahead emergency! Right full rudder!" screamed O'Kane.

The *Tang* had no time to clear out of the torpedo's path. Seconds later a huge explosion rocked the sub, breaking

the air lines and lifting the deck plates. The torpedo had hit the *Tang*'s stern, and there was little time to clear the bridge or even close the hatch before seawater began to rush in. O'Kane and the others on the bridge were washed overboard. The Commander watched in shock and horror as his crippled ship began to sink, stern first, beneath the frothy surface of the Pacific Ocean.

The crewmen trapped inside the *Tang* tried to reach an escape hatch as the submarine settled on the bottom 180 feet below the surface. The *Tang* was taking on water fast, and a severe electrical fire raged out of control. Many of the crew subsequently died from smoke inhalation.

Thirteen of the men attempted to reach the surface using a Mumsen Lung (a special breathing apparatus), but only five succeeded. Meanwhile O'Kane tried to keep the fourteen crew members adrift alongside him, alert until rescue boats arrived. Despite his efforts, only seven others managed to keep afloat until morning. The others either drowned or were taken by sharks.

O'Kane and the other seven (from a total crew of eighty-five) were picked up by an enemy patrol boat and spent the remainder of the war in POW camps. Held first at the secret naval intelligence prison at Ofuna, they were later transferred to the larger camp at Omori.

Liberated on August 28, 1945, O'Kane, severely ill with fever, was hospitalized as a result of his long ordeal. However, his recovery was complete by the time he arrived home in America.

In March of 1946, President Harry Truman presented the Congressional Medal of Honor to Commander Richard O'Kane for his actions in attacking the last two

Japanese convoys in October 1944. The citation read, "For conspicuous gallantry . . . at the risk of his life above and beyond the call of duty. . . . Aided by his gallant command, [O'Kane] achieved an illustrious record of heroism in combat, enhancing the finest traditions of the U.S. Naval Service."

President Truman awarded the *Tang* her second Presidential Unit Citation, one of only three ships in the U.S. Navy to be so honored. In only nine months of service, the *Tang* averaged one enemy ship sunk every eleven days, twice that of any other U.S. submarine. Her twenty-four

The 100th Infantry Battalion serving in Italy during World War II was an all Japanese-American unit of the U.S. Army. On April 4, 1945, Private First Class Sadao Munemori was part of an offensive force moving up the slopes of the Appennino Mountains. Their mission was to capture a hill near Sevarezza held by the enemy.

When the squad leader was wounded, Munemori took command. Scouting alone and ahead of his men, he located a mine field and attacked a German machine gun net with hand grenades. As he returned to his squad, an enemy patrol launched a grenade attack.

One of the grenades bounced off Munemori's helmet and fell into a foxhole occupied by two other U.S. soldiers. Without thought for his own safety, Munemori leaped onto the deadly grenade and smothered the blast with his own body. He was killed instantly, but the other two men survived the explosion.

For his unselfish act of bravery, Sadao Munemori was posthumously awarded the Congressional Medal of Honor.

sinkings ranked the *Tang* in second place behind the *Tautog*, credited with twenty-six sinkings over a period of several years.

Richard O'Kane was considered one of the leading submarine captains of World War II, credited with using innovative and daring tactics in combat situations. O'Kane stayed until his retirement in 1957 to Sebastopol, California. In 1977 he wrote of his experience in *Clear the Bridge—The War Patrols of the U.S.S.* Tang.

O'Kane died on February 16, 1994, at the age of eighty-three. In addition to the Congressional Medal of Honor, he received three Navy Crosses, three Silver Stars, and a Legion of Merit, among other military decorations.

One Against the World

To fully understand Adolph Hitler and the Nazis' rise to power in Germany, one has to go back to the end of the First World War and the defeat of Germany in 1918. The German people resented the terms of the Versailles Treaty of 1919, which limited them militarily and politically. They were forced to pay other countries for damage they caused and surrender any land they had conquered during the war.

The mood of the country was very bitter in the post-war 1920s, but it was the Great Depression, beginning with the stock market crash of 1929, that devastated Germany's economy. Unemployment rose to more than eleven percent of the population, nearly seven million people. Family savings were wiped out and poverty was widespread throughout the country.

It was the Nazi party that claimed to have real solutions to all of Germany's problems. Adolph Hitler summed up what he had done for his country in 1939 when he told President Roosevelt, "I have re-established order . . . increased production . . . found work for the unemployed . . . and rearmed Germany. . . . I have brought back . . . provinces stolen from us in 1919."

In return, most of the German people looked away when their Jewish neighbors were arrested during the night and asked no questions when they were never seen again. The people traded their personal liberty for the so-called stability, prosperity, and control the Nazis offered. But it wasn't long before Germans informed on other Germans, and children informed on their parents. Soon Germany became a police state ruled by fear.

Most Germans took the easy route and remained detached

from the atrocities of the Hitler regime. But some of the brave few opposed Hitler and the Nazis. They fought back quietly with bold and heroic acts on a personal level. Opposing the Nazis took real courage and true valor.

Hiltgunt Zassenhaus

Approaching the gate to the prison in Butzow, Germany, in the fall of 1944, a young blond woman carrying a large, heavy suitcase raised her arm in the Nazi salute, uttering the words, "Heil Hitler," and presenting

Germany

her official papers to the guard. Her name was Fraulein Hiltgunt Zassenhaus of Hamburg, an officer of the Department of Justice. She was traveling under direct orders from the Gestapo.

"This way, please, Fraulein," instructed a guard, pointing to the warden's office.

Hiltgunt was brief and to the point with the warden. "I have here a list of prisoners that I need to question. Please bring them to the visitor's room immediately!"

"Of course, Fraulein. Right away," replied the warden nervously.

Hiltgunt knew they feared her since she was an important official of the Gestapo. What they didn't know was that she feared them even more. For at any moment, they might discover the food, medicine, and correspondence she smuggled in her suitcase for the prisoners. Her life was always in danger, but she gladly took the risk.

In the visitor's room, Hiltgunt sat stone-faced as the thin, sickly, half-starved men were brought in one by one. They were political prisoners from the Danish Resistance, and because Hiltgunt was the only woman in Germany who spoke fluent Danish and Norwegian, she was assigned to interrogate these particular prisoners.

"You may leave us alone now," she declared to the prison guards, who left the room quickly.

Instantly Hiltgunt and the prisoners smiled and exchanged warm hellos. She had special news for Knud Christensen, one of the men. "Congratulations. You have a baby daughter, born on September 4." She showed him a photograph of his wife and new baby waiting for him in Denmark.

The men called her the German Angel, because she gave hundreds of political prisoners of Nazi Germany the will to live and whatever food, supplies, or news she could smuggle in to them.

Born in 1916, Hiltgunt was the daughter of a Lutheran minister and a mother who was an active member of the liberal Social Democrat party. According to Kevin Sim in his book *Women at War*, Hiltgunt and her three brothers were raised in a home where intellectual freedom and individual responsibility were emphasized above all things.

As the Nazi party slowly assumed power throughout Germany, the Zassenhaus family grew firm in their opposition to Hitler and all he stood for. Young Hiltgunt declared that Hitler was a psychotic. By 1933, the psychotic had become Chancellor of Germany.

Hiltgunt was the only one in her class of thirty who refused to give the Nazi salute each morning. Even the four Jewish girls in the class had been convinced to say "Heil Hitler," so as not to draw attention to themselves.

According to Sim, Hiltgunt "never wavered in her belief that individual liberty was worth any sacrifice." But most Germans disagreed. They went along with what the Nazis demanded of them and turned their heads the other way when it became too unpleasant to watch.

As discrimination against Jews increased in Germany, Sim noted that most Germans "preferred to turn a blind eye. . . . In the entire history of the Third Reich, no single body—civic, academic, or even religious—ever made any protest against the regime's inhumanity."

By 1938, the twenty-two-year-old had graduated the University of Hamburg with a degree in Scandinavian

languages. Because of her degree, she was appointed inter-
preter in Danish and Norwegian at the court of Hamburg.
When Hitler invaded Poland in September of 1939, and the
war began, Hiltgunt was ordered to censor all Scandinavian mail. When letters from Jews in Germany were sent to
relatives in Scandinavia, Hiltgunt was ordered to "strike
out any requests for food and clothing."

This job at last gave Hiltgunt an opportunity to oppose
the Nazis. She smuggled letters out and wrote her own
messages to send food and clothing. But one day there
were no longer any letters for Jews, and Hiltgunt suspected
that most of them had been taken away to concentration
camps. She enrolled as a medical student at the university,
which excused her from further work as a censor.

When Hitler invaded and conquered Denmark and
Norway in 1940, Hiltgunt was ordered to work with political prisoners of those countries. Her duties included
censoring their mail and supervising their visits. It was
then that Hiltgunt decided to help the ill and under-
nourished prisoners in every possible way.

According to Sim, Hiltgunt was in contact with over
1,200 Scandinavian prisoners throughout Germany. She became a go-between to their families back home and
brought them home-baked bread, vitamins, pencils and
paper, and letters.

The constant risk to Hiltgunt was tremendous. Death
sentences in Nazi Germany were so common that a person
could be executed for making an anti-Nazi joke. There's no
doubt that if Hiltgunt had been caught, she would have
been killed. Three times she was brought in by the Gestapo

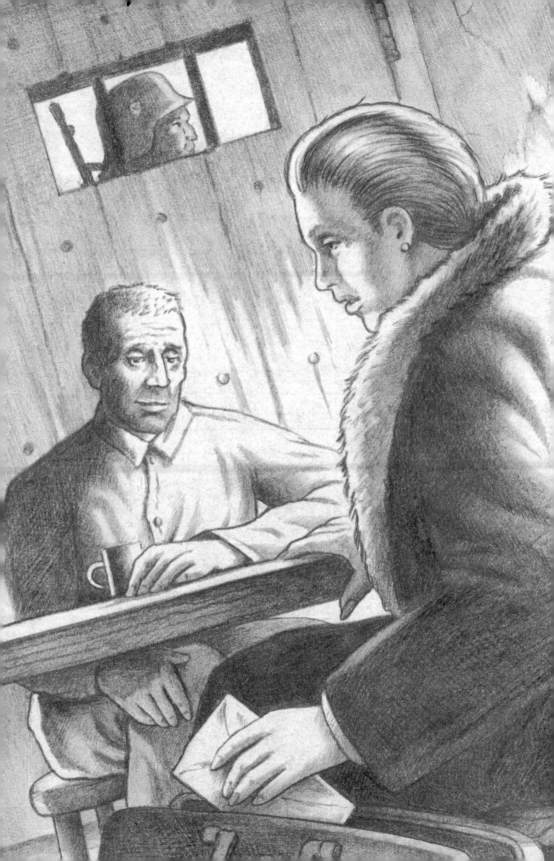

for questioning, and each time she gave the correct answers and was released.

As the war years passed, the tide turned against Germany. The Allies' continuous bombing turned Hiltgunt's home city of Hamburg into rubble. In the summer of 1943, 40,000 were killed in one July week and a million fled the city. Hiltgunt had mixed feelings. She watched the city she loved being destroyed but knew it had to happen if Hitler was to be stopped. "As a German," said Hiltgunt in *Women at War*, "I had to hope continuously for the demise of Nazi Germany."

Opposition to Hitler and his Nazi regime extended into the German military. Leading members of the regular Army were concerned about the evils of Nazism and the danger of eventual defeat. They hoped to negotiate a peaceful end to the war and to avoid complete destruction of their homeland.

Colonel Claus Von Stauffenberg was part of a group of armed officers who attempted to assassinate Hitler on July 20, 1944. The Colonel attended a military briefing in the German war room at Rastenburg. He set his briefcase, filled with explosives, under the table near Hitler and left the room to supposedly make an important phone call.

The bomb exploded moments later. But unfortunately the Nazi leader was only wounded. As fate would have it, another officer had moved the case to the other side of the table. It was this thick table that probably saved Adolf Hitler's life. Von Stauffenberg and the other conspirators were quickly rounded up and executed by the Nazis.

Late in the war, the German people were starving. The average diet in Hamburg consisted mainly of turnips. They often had no gas or electricity. Hiltgunt—exhausted and ill herself—continued to see her prisoners and keep written records of their whereabouts. Often she had to track them down because they had been transferred to other sites in Germany.

Early in 1945, one hostile warden insisted on keeping a guard on Hiltgunt while she was with her prisoners. She had come to love these men, and when she saw their wretched physical condition, instead of using German, she spoke in Norwegian, giving news and messages of support. The guard reported this incident to the warden, who told Hiltgunt she would be reported to the Gestapo for breaking the rules.

This event happened to occur on the same day the Allies bombed the city of Dresden in Germany. There was widespread confusion, and Hiltgunt never knew if the Gestapo was ever made aware of her secret activity.

The end for Germany was near, and the Nazis finally allowed the Red Cross to collect Hiltgunt's Scandinavian prisoners with the help of the written files she had secretly kept.

When the war ended in 1945, Hiltgunt worked with war orphans. She became known as a hero in the Scandinavian countries, and in 1947 she was the first German after the war to be invited to Norway and Denmark.

Bomber Squadron

Once the United States entered the war in December 1941, American servicemen of the 8th Air Force Division arrived in England in early 1942, but it wasn't until the middle of that year that U.S. bombers began to fly regular missions over Europe. As American aircraft productivity increased at home, the Allied air offensive in Europe grew in scope and frequency. By war's end, three hundred thousand aircraft had been involved in the conflict.

Daylight bombing raids over occupied France and Germany intensified, paving the way for the June 6, 1944, landing of Allied troops on the beaches of Normandy, France (on D-Day). Common targets of American-made bombers such as the B-17 Flying Fortress were fuel and industrial factories, airfields, roads, railway lines, bridges, and major urban centers.

The B-17 Flying Fortresses were the workhorses of the war in Europe. The world's first four-engine heavy bomber, the well-built sturdy B-17s often flew deep into German territory on bombing raids. Capable of withstanding considerable punishment, many B-17s returned safely home despite crippled wings, exposed engines, and fuselages riddled with bullet holes.

Forrest Vosler

"Heavy ground fire ahead," shouted twenty-year-old Technical Sergeant Forrest Vosler to the rest of the crew of the B-17 Flying Fortress. "Get ready for a bumpy ride."

Vosler was flying his fourth mission as a radioman/gunner in a bombing raid on Germany, in late December

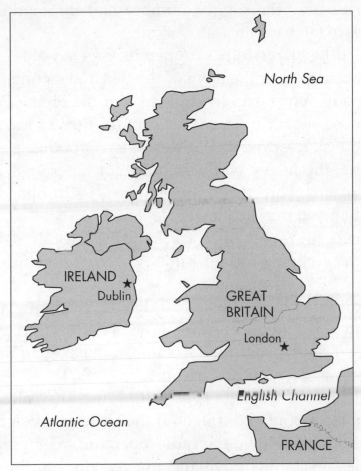

United Kingdom

1943. The men in the bomber squadrons of the 8th Air Force suffered heavy losses aboard these B-17s bound for the heart of enemy territory. Flying in tight formations for protection, without fighter escorts, the bombers were often sitting ducks for faster, more maneuverable enemy fighter planes as well as anti-aircraft ground fire.

Suddenly the big plane shuddered noticeably.

"We've been hit," yelled Vosler. "One of the engines is gone."

Fortunately the rugged bomber had three additional engines to fall back on.

The B-17 successfully dropped its payload of bombs on enemy targets over the town of Bremen and swung around to begin its return trip to England. But the Flying Fortress took a second hit from enemy ground fire, and a second engine was destroyed. With only two good engines remaining, the heavy bomber could not keep up with the other planes. Forced to reduce speed, it dropped out of formation and flew at a lower elevation.

"Keep your eyes open for bandits," declared Vosler, who knew enemy fighter pilots watched specifically for crippled B-17s flying alone.

Suddenly the sky was filled with German Messerschmitts. "We've got visitors, boys. Bandits at two, four, and six o'clock," said the top gunner. "Let's give them an old-fashioned American welcome."

Instantly the gunners began firing the fifty-caliber machine guns mounted throughout the airplane. Vosler's gun was positioned above the radio operator's compartment. The Messerschmitts dove and opened fire on the slower moving B-17. The American gunners returned round after round hoping to fight off the deadly enemy fighters.

Then, without warning, a twenty-millimeter cannon shell from one of the Messerschmitts exploded in the tiny radio compartment. Vosler was hit in the legs and thighs. Hot metal fragments seared his arms and chest. The pain that coursed through his body nearly caused Vosler to lose consciousness.

Vosler was aware that the B-17 had taken a direct hit in the tail section, seriously wounding the tail gunner, so he

crawled back behind his machine gun and resumed his defense of the crippled B-17.

But then another twenty-millimeter shell exploded alongside the determined radio operator. This time Vosler was wounded in the chest and face. Pieces of metal sliced into both of his eyes, blurring his vision. And, although he could barely see, he continued to fire his machine gun until the German fighters finally gave up the fight and turned back.

While Vosler helped the wounded tail gunner, the pilot of the crippled bomber struggled to keep the B-17 in the air until it reached the English Channel. There, he would ditch the plane in the water and pray he and the crew remained unnoticed by the Germans.

Vosler knew that a working radio would be the difference between being rescued or dying in the Channel, but the plane's radio equipment had been destroyed during the fierce air battle. Working almost entirely by his sense of touch, while lapsing in and out of consciousness, Vosler was able to repair the radio and began transmitting a distress signal just as the pilot ditched the B-17 in the Channel.

When the big bomber settled into the water, it began to sink slowly. The crew managed to escape onto one of the B-17's fifty-two-foot-long wings. While some members of the crew readied a life raft, Vosler saw the wounded tail gunner slip off the wing into the water. Despite his injuries, the radioman dove into the water and dragged the tailgunner back onto the wing with one hand. With his other hand he held up the bomber's radio antenna so that the distress signal would continue to be transmitted.

Forrest Vosler remained blind for eight months after the incident. His retinas had been severly damaged by the enemy shell that exploded in his face. One eye had to be removed during surgery, but doctors tried to repair the other eye, hopeful that Vosler would regain some sight with time.

In the meantime Vosler was awarded the Congressional Medal of Honor for the "extraordinary courage, coolness, and skill he displayed in the face of great odds." His actions during and after the bombing run over Bremen, Germany, were an inspiration to the crew members serving alongside him.

The twenty-year-old was set to receive his Medal of Honor in a special ceremony held at the White House. The President of the United States, Franklin Delano Roosevelt, was to present the award to Vosler. But the President

In the early days of the air offensive in Europe, B-17s were unescorted and consequently suffered terrible losses in their bombing raids over Germany. Without fighter protection, bombers were at the mercy of the faster German Messerschmitts.

Top priority was given to developing a long-range, high-altitude fighter plane to escort the bombers. It was the newly upgraded P-51 Mustang that became the first American fighter to venture into Germany. As they began escorting squadrons of heavy bomber formations into the Nazi heartland on a regular basis, Allied bomber losses steadily decreased.

Each Mustang packed six fifty-inch machine guns plus 2,000 pounds of bombs or six five-inch rockets. For every P-51 Mustang shot down in combat, seven German Messerschmitts were destroyed.

purposely delayed the medal ceremony, hoping the courageous radioman would regain his eyesight.

On August 31, 1944, Forrest Vosler was finally presented with the Congressional Medal of Honor—and he was actually able to *see* President Roosevelt as he spoke at the White House. Vosler had regained sight in his remaining eye.

A New York native who had a home in Florida, Forrest Vosler died on February 17, 1992, at the age of sixty-nine. He is buried in Arlington National Cemetery.

An American in Paris

Organized resistance to the German occupation of Europe was encouraged and supported by the Allies during World War II. Such resistance took many forms, including sabotage, espionage, assassinations, and even armed uprisings.

The most successful activities were the publication of underground newspapers, the transmission of intelligence information, and the smuggling out of occupied territory of those airmen who had crashed or parachuted behind enemy lines.

Women played important roles in all resistance activities, especially in work involving escape lines. According to Margaret Rossiter in Women in the Resistance, *five thousand Allied airmen, three thousand of whom were American, were helped to return to their bases in England via escape routes throughout Europe. These lines of escape also gave aid and assistance to free French fighters and Jewish refugees attempting to escape from France.*

Working on escape lines was very dangerous. Large numbers of men and women were arrested and transported to concentration camps as a result of their work.

Virginia d'Albert Lake

"Your identity papers, please," requested the German officer in flawless French. The man and woman standing before him handed over their documents, and the officer scanned them quickly.

He had stopped the two on a routine security check. The couple were bicycling south from the town of

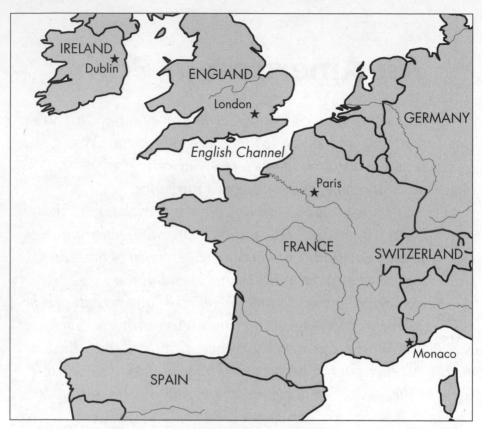

Western Europe

Chateaudun in German-occupied France. It was June 12, 1944, less than a week after the Allies had landed in Normandy in the D-Day invasion.

"What are you doing in Chateaudun, Madame, when your home is in Paris?" the officer asked gruffly.

"I'm looking for eggs and fresh produce," replied the attractive young woman. She spoke French with an obvious American accent.

Then the German saw from her papers that she was born in the United States. The man remained silent, but the officer assumed that he, too, was an American.

"Your pocketbook, please."

The woman handed her purse to the officer, who searched its contents carefully, finding a list of names and a suspiciously large amount of money—more than 100,000 francs.

The officer then turned to speak to the two military companions standing beside him. "I think we've caught ourselves some big fish in the Resistance. Let's take them in for questioning," he said in German.

He handed the woman back her purse. Then one of the other German soldiers grabbed the couple's arms and guided the two into the backseat of a large black car. As the vehicle sped away the woman carefully took the list of names from her purse and tore the sheet of paper into tiny bits that she then hid in her pocket.

The arrested woman was Virginia d'Albert Lake, an active member of the French Resistance and guide in the underground Comet escape line. She helped Allied soldiers and other fugitives evade capture by the Germans by directing them to the Spanish border. The man was an airman named Alfred Hickman, whom Virginia was helping escape from occupied France. Virginia's story is related by Margaret Rossiter in her book *Women in the Resistance*.

Virginia Roush was an ordinary American girl, born in Dayton, Ohio, in 1910. She grew up in St. Petersburg, Florida, and graduated from Rollins College in 1935. On a trip to France in 1936, she met a handsome Frenchman named Philippe d'Albert Lake. The two fell in love.

In 1937, Philippe and Virginia were married and took up residence in Philippe's home in Cancaval, France. Although she would now be living abroad permanently, Virginia decided to maintain her American citizenship. This decision may have saved her life.

When the war broke out, Philippe served in the French military. But after France fell to the Germans in 1940, he returned home. The conquering armies took over the d'Albert Lakes' home in Cancaval, so the two retreated to their apartment in Paris. They also occasionally traveled to a house in the country twenty-four miles outside of the city.

Wealthy by most standards, Virginia and Philippe d'Albert Lake could have lived in relative comfort during the German occupation. But the brutal German regime compelled the couple to action.

While staying at their country house outside Paris in 1943, the local baker asked the couple to meet with three American airmen he was hiding in the bakery. Virginia was delighted to talk with fellow Americans, and the couple decided to work for the Resistance on the Comet escape line.

Soon Philippe was in charge of the Paris sector of the Comet line. Virginia became a safehouse keeper and guide. She picked up airmen, hid and fed them, and provided them with clothing, papers, and even train tickets. She also acted as a liaison to other escape routes. Even though she spoke fluent French, her American accent made it difficult for her to go anywhere without being stopped and searched.

By April 1944 the d'Albert Lakes became involved in organizing a hidden camp for Allied airmen in the densely wooded forest of Freteval, seven miles south of Chateaudun. Clearings in the woods not far from the campsite were ideal spots for parachute drops.

Before long Comet guides began escorting airmen to the hidden camp, where they lived in camouflaged tents. Local men and women helped in the effort to feed, clothe, and care for the men who often suffered from serious injuries.

With the Allied landings in Normandy, the d'Albert Lakes decided to abandon their Paris apartment and hide in the camp until they could be liberated by the advancing Allies. They were in the midst of escorting eleven airmen to Freteval when the two split up to guide their charges on foot for the remaining miles of the trek.

With eighteen miles to go, the six airmen, accompanied by Virginia, were too weak to continue, so she bicycled ahead to Chateaudun and obtained a cart from other Resistance members. She was driving the cart with its valuable hidden human cargo when she and airman Alfred Hickman were stopped by the Germans.

Sitting in the backseat of the German's car, Virginia could only think of one thing: No matter what happened, she would not betray the people in Chateaudun or other members of the Resistance. That's why she'd torn the list of contacts into little pieces.

The two prisoners were taken directly to Gestapo (Nazi secret police) headquarters in Chateaudun. Virginia was left unguarded for a few seconds, and she quickly retrieved the torn bits of paper from her pocket and swallowed each and every one of them.

Transported to the next prison at Fresnes outside Paris, she was separated from Hickman, whom Virginia would never see again. She was confined to a small cell for nearly two months and questioned extensively each day.

Despite constant badgering and pressure, Virginia did

not break down at any time. She held up under constant questioning and never betrayed a single Resistance worker or Allied airman.

On August 15, with the Allies just west of Paris, Virginia was forced into a dirty, crowded railroad boxcar with other prisoners. Her journey temporarily ended at the Ravensbruck concentration camp after a hellish 144-hour trip. Over the course of the next nine months, Virginia spent time in two other camps in Eastern Europe. She was slowly starved and overworked, left without warm clothes and shoes, and forced to sleep with three or four other prisoners in a single bunk.

By February of 1945, Virginia's physical condition had deteriorated. She weighed seventy-six pounds (down from 126 pounds), and her skin was covered with lice and open sores. The German officers in the camp—realizing the war was lost—began to believe that it was in their best interest to treat prisoners better, especially Americans. As part of this special treatment, Virginia was given flea powder and a warm coat and then transferred to Liebenau, a Red Cross camp.

With their widespread participation in the Resistance movement, the women of France finally earned the right to be full citizens of their country. They voted for the very first time in April 1945, leaving Switzerland the only western country after World War II that denied women the right to vote. It wasn't until 1971 that Swiss women were finally granted that right.

According to Roster, Virginia said, "If I had spent one more week . . . I would have died like my friends."

Liberated by French troops on April 21, Virginia arrived in Paris on May 27, 1945, and was reunited with her husband. She was lucky to be alive.

The men at the forest camp at Freteval (more than thirty airmen) were all rescued by the Allies. Virginia personally helped sixty-seven airmen hide from the Germans and escape from occupied France. To the many men she helped and the dozens who worked alongside her, Virginia d'Albert Lake was a hero.

She received many awards after the war, including the Croix de Guerre and the Medal of the Resistance from France, the Order of the British Empire from Britain, and the Medal of Freedom from America.

Commando

The first real test for American soldiers on the European front came in North Africa in 1943. American forces under General George Patton joined with British forces under General Bernard Montgomery to defeat and drive the Germans from Tunisia.

The next step was an Allied invasion of Italy in an effort to force the Italian government out of the war. After victory was achieved in Sicily, Italy, the Allies landed at Salerno Beach, Italy in September of 1943. Following fierce fighting in the hills around Salerno, Americans liberated Naples and then made their way to Rome. But it took ten months and some of the fiercest and bloodiest battles of the war to liberate Italy's capital city.

The Italian campaign consisted of small-scale, bitter battles waged from one hill ridge to the next and from one small village to another. As the fighting stretched into the winter months, the cold, wind, and rain made each day seem like an eternity for the ordinary foot soldier.

On June 4, 1944, American forces entered Rome to the grateful cheers of Italian citizens. Two days later waves of Allied troops stormed the beaches of Normandy, and the long-awaited invasion of France had begun. Within a year the Allies would retake France and force the Germans back to their own borders.

As British and American troops pressed forward into Germany from the west, and the Russians penetrated the Nazi heartland from the east, the end of the war was within sight. By late April of 1945, Berlin had fallen, Hitler had committed suicide, and all German resistance ceased. May 8, 1945, was declared Victory in Europe (VE) Day.

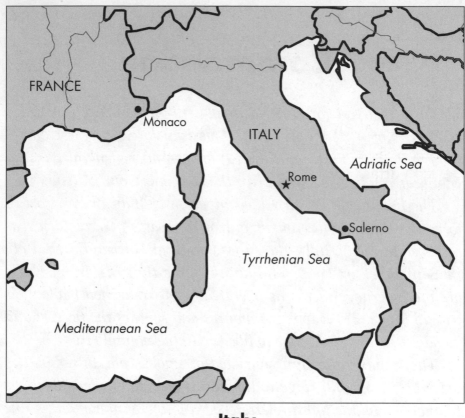

Italy

Charles Kelly

September 13, 1943, turned out to be one of the busiest days in Corporal Charles Kelly's entire life. Several days earlier, Charles's 36th "Texas" Infantry Division had landed on Salerno Beach, Italy, and advanced slowly inland despite heavy German artillery and mortar fire.

On this particularly hot and sunny morning near Altavilla, Italy, Charles volunteered to join a patrol that located and then eliminated two enemy machine-gun nests. Then, under heavy gunfire, he scouted German-held Hill 315. After an unexpected confrontation with a German combat control in which Charles traded fire with the enemy, he returned to his unit and reported his findings.

By this time, Charles's ammunition was exhausted, and he was sent to Altavilla for more.

The Altavilla's mayor's three-story house was being used as an ammunition and weapons storehouse by the Americans. When Charles arrived, it was under heavy German attack on all sides. The windows were barricaded with mattresses. Inside, U.S. forces were determined to hold out as long as possible.

Charles suddenly found himself participating in the defense of the building. It was an American island in a sea of German artillery and sniper fire. American GIs fought back from every window of the house. Charles took up a position at a second-floor window and started firing. Four German soldiers toppled over dead after his first burst of gunfire.

Charles was soon assigned the task of protecting the rear of the storehouse. Throughout the afternoon and into the night, the twenty-three-year-old fired to keep the enemy back until the barrel grew so red-hot, it locked and wouldn't work anymore. Charles tossed it on a bed in the house, and it started a small fire on the blanket. Then he grabbed a tommy gun and continued shooting until he ran out of ammunition.

American casualties were mounting steadily, especially among those GIs defending the windows. Then there was silence, a lull in the fighting, and Charles found himself alone. The other GIs lay dead, crumpled against the wall or laid out on the ammo-strewn floor around him. Charles had to figure out what to do next, how to save his own life and help the Allied cause.

Charles Kelly was born on September 23, 1920, in Pittsburgh, Pennsylvania, and grew up in a poor neighborhood. The Kellys and their nine children lived in a small shack in an alley behind a tenement building. They had no electricity and no indoor plumbing.

Charles had a difficult childhood. He left school after the eighth grade and hung around street corners getting into trouble. He was headed on a one-way track to nowhere when the war broke out in 1941. The twenty-year-old immediately joined the army. He was described as a sloppy soldier, but an excellent marksman.

At first, Charles volunteered to be a paratrooper. Then he became depressed about his decision and went AWOL (absent without leave), back to Pittsburgh. He returned after a few weeks to take his punishment and was court-martialed by the Army. After a month of restriction and a fine, Charles was transferred to the 36th "Texas" Infantry Division. There he found a home among the tough, high-spirited Texans. On the rifle range, no one cared how he sighted his rifle, as long as he hit the target. Charles Kelly was shipped overseas with the 36th and landed on Salerno Beach, where he got more than his share of combat experience.

Some of the fiercest fighting came at the artillery house at Altavilla. Before long, the silence Charles had experienced ended. The fighting resumed. Wave after wave of Germans surrounded and attacked the house, but Charles never let up. When there was no more ammunition for the rocket launcher, he tossed an incendiary grenade on the roof of a nearby building that was sheltering dozens of enemy troops. Trembling, Charles watched as the building burst into flames.

He got to his feet and looked out a window. Glancing down, he noticed German soldiers advancing on the house from an adjacent alleyway. Charles knew he had to do something quickly. He saw some containers of sixty-millimeter mortar shells nearby. These were powerful and dangerous weapons, not meant to be launched by hand. He had no choice. Charles knew the shell's safety pin controlled the charge and cap inside, and without hesitation, the young corporal pulled the pin and threw the live shell out the window onto the advancing Germans below. The blast was deafening, but it stopped the Germans in their tracks. Charles felt relief; he felt proud. The Army had

American GIs during World War II often served in combat for years at a time before going home. Some soldiers were involved in successive campaigns in North Africa, Italy, and France with only an occasional leave. Front-line troops were involved in the war twenty-four hours a day, seven days a week.

Life for the typical infantry soldier involved digging trenches, endless marches, and exhaustion from lack of sleep—all of this with the specter of death constantly looming over their heads. In the winter months, bad weather conditions added to the soldier's physical discomfort in the field.

GIs ate canned rations and had no hot water or hot meals. Soldiers never took off their clothes (except for their shoes) regardless of how wet and cold they were. Most were lonely, homesick young men in their late teens and twenties. Yet as war correspondent Ernie Pyle once said, "They were the guys that wars can't be won without. . . ."

given him an opportunity to make a difference, to prove his worth. Although he feared for his life, he felt that his actions might actually help the cause.

After Altavilla, Charles served seven months of hard combat in Italy. He returned to his old hometown a hero and a Medal of Honor winner.

After the war, Charles was paid a substantial amount of money by a Hollywood producer for the rights to a movie about his life. Charles used this money to buy his parents a new home with electricity and indoor plumbing.

Charles "Commando" Kelly died in 1985 at the age of 65.

The Young Medic

On April 1, 1945, the battle began between American and Japanese forces for the island of Okinawa in the Pacific Ocean. It was a crucial battle for both sides. The Americans had already gained the upper hand in the war, and victory at Okinawa would most certainly lead to an invasion of the Japanese home islands. The Japanese, their dreams of empire dissolving before their eyes, were well aware of the strategic importance of Okinawa, part of the Ryukyu Island chain, and they would use every means possible to defend it.

Kamikaze fighters crashed their planes into nearby American surface ships in suicidal attacks. Baka bombs, or "human guided missiles," were also used against the Americans—tiny gliders with rocket boosters and 3,000-pound warheads piloted by young men anxious to give up their lives for Japan's Emperor Hirohito.

The ground fighting on Okinawa was among the bloodiest and most vicious of the war. In the caves, pillboxes, and fortified hills of the southern part of this island the battle dragged on for nearly three months. According to those who were fortunate enough to survive Okinawa, it was the most brutal, despairing, and unforgettable experience of their lives.

Robert Eugene Bush

The sky was bursting with the sights and sounds of war. Artillery, mortar, and machine gunfire showered down on the 2nd Battalion rifle company as they attempted to

70

Japan and Korea

take control of the southern half of Okinawa Island. U.S. Marines had already taken the northern half of the island, having met with little resistance, but the south was another story. Realizing that losing Okinawa would probably lead to an attack on their home islands, the Japanese were not going to give up without a fight. Grenades exploded everywhere, and the screams and moans of the wounded rose up from the battlefield like smoke from a funeral pyre.

It was a wet and chilly morning, and nineteen-year-old Robert Eugene Bush, a medical corpsman with the 2nd Battalion, took in the horrors that lay before him with utter dread and dismay. He had no way of knowing that he was standing right in the middle of one of the largest and bloodiest battles of the Pacific War.

Everything had happened so suddenly for the teenager from Washington State. One minute he was aboard a transport boat, chatting with his buddies from the 2nd Battalion as they skimmed over the placid Pacific Ocean. The next thing he knew he was in the thick of battle on Okinawa Island, dead and wounded marines everywhere. As was his duty, the young medic lagged behind the advancing marines and scanned the battlefield for those who needed medical assistance.

The explosion of gunfire was deafening, and the sky teemed with hot, white tracer fire and billowing gray-black clouds.

The medic's mind wandered, and he began thinking about his family, his friends . . .

A nearby explosion rattled his bones and brought him back to the harsh present. He looked up at the burnt remains of a huge palm frond spiraling to the ground by his feet. Bush knew this was no time to think about the past, nor was there any time to consider just how perilous the present situation was. There were wounded men out there, who were barely alive, who needed his attention. Taking a deep breath, he rushed into the open field and began moving from one casualty to the next, his upper body bent forward toward the ground.

The Geneva Convention Code (a series of rules and

regulations concerning nations at war) that protected the lives of medics in the field of battle had long been abandoned on Okinawa, as Robert and others were well aware. But the medic attended to the downed men regardless, doing his best to hug the ground as he tried to stay close to the marines who led the way about one hundred yards ahead of him.

As the American soldiers advanced over a ridge, Robert Eugene Bush was following closely behind when he spotted a lone marine lying face down in a puddle. The medic stopped in his tracks, sensing the danger of being exposed on the elevated ridge. Snipers had been known to hide behind the thick-trunked palms and inside the caves that tunneled throughout the rocky island. From his present position, Robert knew he was a sitting duck. Nevertheless he got down into a crouch, wrapped his arm tightly around his medical bag, and started off toward the downed marine.

"I'm here to help you, sir," the medic yelled, kneeling down beside the officer. The marine had lost a lot of blood, so Robert checked his pulse and was relieved to find him still alive. Immediately he began administering blood plasma in an effort to save the man's life. "Don't worry, sir," he said. "I'll get you out of here." He continued talking, trying to ease the wounded man's pain and fright, even though the medic doubted his words could be heard over the explosive din of warfare.

Holding the glass bottle of plasma aloft in one hand, Bush was a clear target when about twenty enemy soldiers suddenly emerged from the thick brush off to the side and launched a small but potentially lethal counterattack. Without hesitation, the teenager drew his pistol with

his free hand and fired at the enemy until his ammunition was gone.

Then it happened—a loud pop, followed by the sound of shattering glass. Robert Eugene Bush felt pain like never before in his nineteen years of life. An enemy bullet had smashed the plasma bottle, blinding him in one eye and severely lacerating the rest of his face. Out of ammo, the enemy closing in on his position, the young medic ignored the terrible pain and with his good eye managed to spot a discarded rifle lying on the ground several feet away.

If he had any chance of saving the officer and himself, he would have to help fight off the enemy, six of whom were presently charging in his direction.

In one fluid motion he grabbed the weapon from the ground, knelt in front of the disabled officer, and began firing on the advancing soldiers.

Somehow Robert Eugene Bush managed to fend off the enemy while protecting the marine by his feet. All six enemy soldiers lay dead or wounded in his path, and the counterattack had been stopped in its tracks.

With blood streaming down his face, Robert administered another bottle of plasma to the unconscious marine and waited for stretcher bearers to arrive and take the officer to a field hospital.

When help finally came, one of the corpsmen took one look at Robert's face and gasped. "You need immediate medical attention!" the man exclaimed.

"No, I'm all right," Bush replied. "But this patient has to be evacuated immediately!"

Once the wounded officer was carried away, Bush insisted on walking to the battle aid station without assistance.

Halfway there he fell to the ground, unconscious.

Robert Eugene Bush lost an eye as a result of the battle of Okinawa. But he managed to save several lives despite his injury, including the officer from the ridge. He was later awarded the Congressional Medal of Honor and was the youngest Navy recipient of the award in World War II. His citation read, "For conspicuous gallantry . . . at the risk of his life above and beyond the call of duty. His daring initiative, great personal valor, and heroic spirit of self-sacrifice in service of others reflect great credit upon Bush and enhance the finest traditions of the U.S. Naval Service."

With the capture of Okinawa by the Americans, plans were undertaken to prepare for an attack on the island in the Japanese archipelago. Many military strategists believed the Japanese would fight to the last man, thus extending the length of the war for perhaps another year and requiring a massive American land force invasion of Japan. But in August of 1945, two atomic bombs were dropped on the Japanese cities of Hiroshima and Nagasaki. The tragedy and devastation caused by these nuclear weapons effectively ended the war, leading to Japan's official surrender on September 2, 1945.

Okinawa was the last great battle of World War II.

Glossary

ADVERSARY: opponent, enemy

AERONAUTICAL: dealing with the science or art of flight

ALLY: one that helps or joins another in a common cause

ANTI-SEMITIC: an unreasonable dislike or fear of Jews; *see* Prejudice

ARCHIPELAGO: a group or chain of islands

ARSENAL: a place for storing weapons and ammunition

ATROCITIES: shocking and cruel acts

BAYONETS: steel knife attached to muzzle of a rifle

BRIDGE: the raised platform of a ship or submarine for the commanding officer

CANOPY: enclosure over an airplane cockpit

CLARIFY: to make clear and easy to understand

COLLABORATOR: a person who cooperates or works with the enemy

CONJUNCTION: in combination with

CONNING TOWER: the low armored observation and control tower in a submarine

CONVOY: a formation of ships usually accompanied by a protective escort

COURT-MARTIAL: a military court empowered to decide cases involving military personnel accused of violating military law

DISTRESS: suffering, pain, anxiety

ESPIONAGE: spying on others

FORMIDABLE: hard to handle or overcome; dreaded; feared

FRANC: the French monetary unit

FUSELAGE: the main body of an airplane

GENOCIDE: planned extermination of a national or racial group

GESTAPO: secret state police of Nazi Germany

HULL: the frame or body of a ship

HUMANE: tenderness and compassion for the suffering

IDEOLOGICAL: concerned with doctrines or a particular way of thinking of a certain group

IMPOSITION: the forcing of something on another; a requirement

INCENDIARY: used for setting things on fire

INFANTRY: soldiers who fight on foot

INFRACTION: violation, breach, break

INHUMANE: lacking kindness or compassion for the suffering

INITIATIVE: taking the first step or move, originating new ideas or methods

INNOVATIVE: something new or different

INTERNMENT: a condition of being held or confined against one's will

LENIENT: gentle; merciful; mild

MANIFEST: to make clear or evident; show plainly; reveal

NEUTRALITY: the policy of a nation of not taking either side in a war

OMINOUS: threatening; menacing

PAYLOAD: cargo (of bombs)

PERIMETER: the outer border or boundary of an area

PILLBOX: small concrete structure that encloses and protects machine guns

PIVOTAL: of very great importance

PLASMA: the liquid part of blood

PREJUDICE: an unfavorable feeling or opinion formed without knowledge or reason

PSYCHOANALYST: a specialist in treating disorders of the mind

RATIFY: approve; support; endorse

RATIONS: daily allowance of food for servicemen in the field

REPEL: to drive or force back; *see* Repulse

REPULSE: to drive back; *see* Repel

RUDDER: device for steering a ship or airplane

SABOTAGE: intentional destruction or damage of machinery, factories, roads, or bridges by enemy agents in time of war

SAMURAI: warrior class in feudal Japan

SATURATION: the covering or soaking of something completely

SHRAPNEL: shell fragments

SNIPER: a hidden sharpshooter who uses a long-range rifle to shoot at individuals

SOLITARY: alone; without companions

STOCK: the part of a rifle or firearm that holds the barrel

STRAFE: attack with gunfire, especially from low-flying aircraft

TENEMENT: overcrowded apartment building in poorer section of city

TORRENTIAL: rushing, violent streams of water; violent downpour of rain

Bibliography

Appleman, Roy E. and James M. Burns, Russel A. Gugeler, and John Stevens. *Okinawa—The Last Battle*. Rutland, Vermont and Tokyo, Japan: Charles E. Tuttle Company, 1964.

Baldwin, Hanson. *Battles Lost and Won—Great Campaigns of World War II*. New York: Harper & Row Publisher, 1966.

Block, Gay, and Malka Drucker. *Rescuers*. New York: Holmes & Merier Publishers, Inc., 1992.

Congressional Medal of Honor Society—National Headquarters. 40 Patriots Point Road, Mt. Pleasant, South Carolina 29464. Michael Williams, Director. Biographical information.

Cooke, Donald E. *For Conspicuous Gallantry*. Maplewood, New Jersey: C. S. Hammond & Company, 1966.

Garraty, John A., and Peter Gay, eds. *The Columbia History of the World*. New York: Harper & Row Publishers, 1972.

Hersey, John, and Peter Wright. *Manzanar*. New York: Times Books, 1988.

Isserman, Maurine. *America at War—World War II*. New York: Facts on File, 1991.

Jacobs, Bruce. *Heroes of the Army*. New York: W. W. Norton & Company, 1956.

Keegan, John. *The Second World War*. New York: Penguin Books, 1989.

Kerr, E. Bartlett. *Surrender and Survival*. New York: William Morrow and Company, 1985.

Manning, Robert, ed. *Great Events of the 20th Century*. Pleasantville, New York: The Reader's Digest Association, Inc.,1977.

Nardo, Don. *World War II—The War in the Pacific*. San Diego, California: Lucent Books, 1991.

New York Times—Page One (No author given). New York: The New York Times Company, 1983.

O'Kane, Richard. *Clear the Bridge*. New York: Rand McNally & Company, 1977.

Rossiter, Margaret L. *Women in the Resistance*. New York: Praeger Publishers, 1986.

Saywell, Shelley. *Women in War*. New York: Viking, 1985.

Schott, Joseph L. *Above and Beyond*. New York: G. P. Putnam's Sons, 1963.

Sherrod, Robert. *History of Marine Corps Aviation in World War II*. Baltimore, Maryland: The Nautical & Aviation Publishing Co. of America, 1987.

Sim, Kevin. *Women at War*. New York: William Morrow and Company, 1982.

Vail, John J. *World War II—The War in Europe*. San Diego, California: Lucent Books, 1991.